SIMPLE SOUPS

SIMPLE SOUPS

Sixty Shortcut Recipes for Every Occasion

TERESA KENNEDY

Crown Trade Paperbacks
New York

Published by Crown Trade Paperbacks, 201 East 50th Street, New York, New York 10022. Member of the Crown Publishing Group.

Random House, Inc. New York, Toronto, London, Sydney, Auckland

CROWN TRADE PAPERBACKS and colophon are trademarks of Crown Publishers, Inc.

Manufactured in the United States of America

Design by Howard Klein

Library of Congress Cataloging-in-Publication Data

Kennedy, Teresa.
Simple soups: sixty shortcut recipes for every occasion/by Teresa Kennedy.—1st ed.
p. cm.
Includes index
1. Soups. 2. Quick and easy cookery. I. Title.
TX757.K345   1995
641.8'13—dc20   94-21969
CIP

ISBN 0-517-88225-6

10 9 8 7 6 5 4 3 2

For my mother, from whom I inherited the notion

that soup is the finest meal there is

CONTENTS

SIMPLE SOUPS

INTRODUCTION

One of the great mysteries of the wide, wonderful world of cooking is that many people are just plain scared of making soup from scratch. I honestly don't know why, for to me, soup recipes constitute some of the easiest, most flexible, and fun-to-make additions to the cook's repertoire.

Oh, come now, you're saying to yourselves— what about roasting all those bones to make stock? What about hunting down all those scary ingredients like, well—barley? What about the hours and hours it takes to make the stuff? To say nothing of those gallons of leftovers! If I make soup, you say suspiciously, what else will we have on the menu?

Truth is, soup has gotten a very bad reputation among many home cooks who, despite the evidence, insist on thinking of these marvelous concoctions as nothing more than a first course—a throwaway—something made not as the main event, but merely to tempt the appetite for the courses that are to come.

To those cooks, those soup snobs, I say—get real. The seven-course meal—in many instances, the three-course meal—has gone the way of fins on Cadillacs and all those June Cleaver types who wore high heels to sweep the floors and spent their days not only cooking, but actually planning meals. Today's lifestyles, budgets, and eating habits just don't allow for such luxuries. Seriously, when was the last time you planned a week's worth of meals?

The good news is that we don't have to give up the simple pleasures. Hot or cold, creamy or steamily swimming with all sorts of little surprises, soup remains one of the most satisfying meals anyone can prepare.

Did I say meal? I did, and meant it. For the right soup can be the centerpiece of anyone's feast, anytime. Add a glass of wine, a salad, a crusty loaf of fresh bread—and presto! You have a meal fit for the snobbiest of soup snobs, the finickiest of the pickiest.

Soup is good food, and one of the best and healthiest ways to take in all those essential nutrients, fibers, or food groups in one, easy-to-make bowlful.

Soups are economical: they stretch ingredients, and are a wonderful way to use up all those odds and ends that tend to accumulate in the refrigerator. Most of the recipes in this book can be made literally in minutes, and they store beautifully in the refrigerator or freezer. Modern aficionados of soup know the secrets of canned stocks and broths and know, too, that these products are now available in all-natural and low-sodium varieties.

For the real purists among you, however, I've included a couple of basic, all-purpose stock recipes that serve to demystify and modernize the making of homemade stocks, including a few secret shortcuts you may not have come across before. These stocks can be made in batches and frozen in smaller portions for the next time the urge for a bowl of homemade soup overtakes you, like Marcel Proust with a yen for madeleines.

Which brings us to the last and most important feature of homemade soup: comfort. For even more than its food, nutrient, and economic value, soup is guaranteed comfort food. To chase away the chills, to lift the spirits, to warm the heart, there's something in the secret alchemy of homemade soup that's better for your head than a call from Mom or months of psychoanalysis. Soup is food for the spirit as well as the body, and for all of that, it may as well be the food of the gods.

ABOUT SOUP BASES, BROTHS, AND STOCKS

The traditional approach to making soup would have us all believe that long-simmered concoctions of roasted bones and bouquets of various spices are essential to really good soup. While homemade soup stock is still the best, the truth is, a perfectly acceptable stock can come out of a can, be mixed up from bouillon cubes, or even made from leftover gravy and water! Face it, one of the deep, dark secrets of the culinary world is—pardon the cliché—if you can boil water, you can make great soup!

What is essential to good soup stock is that it be flavorful. So, if you're using canned stock, I recommend, first and foremost, that you taste it. Is it on the watery side? Add half a bouillon cube to boost the flavor a bit, or combine it with another can of the same stuff, set it on a burner, and simmer until the stock or broth is reduced by one-third. The reduction process will concentrate the flavor.

When using canned soup stock or broth, shop around. Don't confine yourself to a brand you're less than completely satisfied with, simply because it's there. Excellent low-sodium and all-natural canned broths and stocks can be found in your local health food store, for example. Also note that in the recipes I've included here, the words *broth* or *stock* are used interchangeably.

If you prefer to use bouillon cubes or powder to make your soup base, do experiment with these as well. In general they tend to be higher in salt content than other soup bases, but again, to meet the demands of diet trends, health-conscious companies are coming out with low-sodium, high-flavor alternatives all the time. Now available are vegetable stocks, fish, and even imitation chicken and beef flavors, all good stock alternatives when you and yours prefer a vegetarian menu. Basic powdered or dry soup mixes, especially onion and vegetable flavors, are also excellent bases for stock or broth.

Still, in the end, there's just no substitute for a good homemade soup stock. It's healthier because the individual cook controls things like the amount of fat and salt that go into the broth, and it's economical because one big batch can be frozen in one- or two-cup containers and used in an infinite variety of soups. But contrary to more traditional types, I'm an advocate for the use of shortcuts in cooking, as long as they don't result in a compromise of flavor or quality. Making up a batch of really good soup stock doesn't have to be scary, tedious, or time-consuming. Nor does it require any particular cooking expertise. So, with all that demystification out of the way, let's get down to basics.

WHAT YOU REALLY NEED TO MAKE SOUP STOCK

The following ingredients are used in every soup stock known to humankind. Why? I'm not sure, except that all simmered together, they make for that ineffable combination of flavors that makes great soup.

Water
Carrots
Celery
Onions
Garlic
Salt
Black peppercorns or freshly ground black pepper

If you want to get a bit more creative, choose from the following: bay leaf; green pepper; leeks; parsley; and celery or cabbage hearts, all of which make nice additions to stock, but really aren't essential.

Okay, now for the specifics. You will see that most soup recipes call for a particular flavor of stock.

Chicken Stock
To make chicken stock, for example, you're going to need some chicken parts—bones, wings, backs, the remains of last night's chicken dinner, whatever. The exact nature of the parts used is not really so

important, but keep in mind that some give more flavor to a broth or stock than others. Skin gives more flavor than bones, dark meat more flavor than white, and the bonier (rather than meatier) your soup bones, the longer simmering time they will require to release their flavor. If you're making stock from leftovers, cooked meat and bones require longer simmering to release their flavor than uncooked meat and bones.

Beef Stock When making beef stocks, you definitely need bones, a little bit of fat (don't worry, it can be skimmed off after cooking), and some meat. Keep an eye out for beef soup bones in the supermarket, or get them from your butcher at very little cost. Choose bones that have enough meat and fat on them to impart a good flavor to the soup without hours of simmering. If you wish, the meat can be cut from the bones after cooking, and diced and added to your soup. Beef shins are excellent, marrow bones are unsurpassed in flavor, and for a really hearty, concentrated beef broth, use oxtails. Note that commercial beef stocks will be browner than the ones you produce on the back burner. Tradition would have us believe that this lovely color is imparted from roasted, caramelized bones and vegetables. In the real world, however, your canned stock more than likely gets this lovely color from food coloring. Never fear—if you prefer a browner look to your beef stock, a dash of Worcestershire sauce will do it, and add a nice flavor as well.

Ham Stock Ham stocks can be a little tricky to make—almost no one has a huge ham bone sitting around in the refrigerator. Nonetheless, a lovely ham or pork stock can be made in far less quantity simply by using smoked knuckles or pork neck bones, widely available in supermarkets or from your butcher. After use in the stock, they require some trimming but will usually yield at least some meat to add to your soup.

Fish Stock Fish stocks can be made from fish heads and tails, shrimp shells and heads, bottled clam juice, drainings from cans of water-packed tuna fish or oysters, fresh oyster liquor, and just about anything suitably fish-flavored—including, of course, a few pieces of fresh fish. You can also make a fish stock by cooking the fish of your choice in a vegetable stock, or in some good white wine, which will serve just as well. In general though, soups and chowders containing fish or shellfish take on enough flavor from these ingredients and therefore don't require additional flavoring in the stock.

Vegetable Stock Vegetable stocks can be made from any combination of vegetables, the leftover cooking liquid from vegetables, trimmings from broccoli, celery hearts, or even that cauliflower left over from last week. When making vegetable stocks, however, be sure to include something from the cabbage or broccoli family for maximum soup power and flavor. Collard greens, brussels sprouts, turnip or mustard greens, and mushrooms also add flavor and vitamins. Always consider the flavor of the vegetable before adding it to the vegetable stock. The mild taste of zucchini or summer squash, for instance, might be a lovely addition to a soup, but it won't contribute much in the way of flavor to the stock.

THE ONLY ALL-PURPOSE SOUP STOCK RECIPE YOU WILL EVER NEED

All you need to complete your knowledge of stocks is a basic recipe. Experiment with the one below by adding, subtracting, or seasoning as you desire.

1½ pounds parts (chicken parts for chicken stock, beef bones for beef stock, ham bone or hocks for ham stock, fish for fish stock, or assorted vegetables for vegetable stock)

3 quarts water

2 large onions, diced

3 celery stalks with leaves, diced

4 to 5 scrubbed, unpeeled carrots, diced

3 large garlic cloves, peeled and pressed

3 bay leaves

1 tablespoon salt, or to taste

6 to 8 black peppercorns

Place all the ingredients in a large saucepan or stockpot and bring to a boil over high heat. Cover, reduce the heat to low, and simmer for 1 hour.

Strain the stock through a sieve or colander into another kettle. Return to the burner, turn heat to medium, and boil until the broth is reduced by one third. Use as desired, or divide into 2-cup portions and freeze for up to 6 months.

Makes 10 cups, or enough for 3 to 4 batches of soup

TRADITIONAL BEEF STOCK

For the hard-core traditionalists among you, here is a traditional stock recipe, the whole nine yards. While it is arguably worth the effort to make a large batch of stock two or three times a year and store it in the freezer, be forewarned. This is more than just a recipe. This is a project.

10	pounds meaty beef bones, cracked and cut into 2-inch pieces
3	medium onions, unpeeled and coarsely chopped
3	carrots, unpeeled and cut into chunks
6 to 8	garlic cloves, peeled and coarsely chopped
2	celery stalks, with leaves, cut into chunks
3	large leeks, white parts only, washed and cut into chunks
2	large tomatoes, quartered
6	quarts plus 2 cups of water
6	sprigs fresh thyme
1	tablespoon coarse sea salt
10 to 15	black peppercorns

Preheat the oven to 450° F.

Place the bones in a large roasting pan and roast uncovered for 25 minutes, turning occasionally to ensure even browning. Add the vegetables and continue roasting for an additional 30 minutes, or until bones and vegetables are dark brown but not burned.

Transfer the bones and vegetables to a large stockpot. Add 1½ cups of the water to the roasting pan and place over medium heat for 5 to 10 minutes, stirring and scraping any bits from the bottom of the pan. Add the liquid to the bones and vegetables.

Add the remaining water to the stockpot, and bring to a boil over high heat. Add the thyme, salt, and peppercorns. Reduce heat to low and simmer, uncovered, for 4½ hours, or until the liquid is reduced by approximately one-third.

Strain the stock through a fine sieve into a large container. Pour into another large pot, or return to the stockpot after rinsing the pot thoroughly.

Simmer stock over low heat an additional 2½ to 3 hours, or until it is again reduced by one-third. Cool, divide into containers, and freeze for up to 6 months.

Makes ½ gallon

Chilled Avocado Soup • Chilled Cucumber Soup

Curried Zucchini Soup • Easy Gazpacho

Cold Dill and Shrimp Soup • Green Summer Soup

Summer Sunset Soup • Mixed Berry Soup

Cold Strawberry Soup • Kiwi Soup

Melon Madness • Cream of Mango Soup

COLD AND REFRESHING SOUPS

When summer rolls around, bringing long, lazy days and lighter appetites, nothing is more satisfying than chilled soup, whether it is the main course for a light lunch or supper, or a luscious fruit concoction for dessert. Most of the following recipes can be made in only minutes, are low in fat and calories—perfect for the swimsuit season—and make wonderful use of the freshness of summer's bounty.

Cold soups are light, easy, fresh, and economical. Who could ask for anything more? So, turn off the stove, pad out to the patio, and bask in the glow as your family and guests compliment the cooking.

CHILLED AVOCADO SOUP

Serve this in scooped-out avocado shells, top with a dollop of sour cream, and sprinkle with a combination of black and red caviar for a really special presentation.

- 3 medium avocados
- ½ cup dry white wine
- 2 eggs, soft-boiled (3 to 4 minutes)
- ¾ cup chicken stock, homemade (see page 25) or canned
- 1 cup plain yogurt
  Milk
  Generous dash of hot sauce to taste
- 1 cup sour cream
- 1 ounce caviar (optional)

Slice avocados in half lengthwise, so that they will rest evenly on a plate. Discard the pits and scoop out the pulp, leaving a ⅛- to ¼-inch shell. Cover with plastic wrap and place in the refrigerator.

Place the pulp, wine, eggs, and stock in a food processor or blender. Process until very smooth. Add the yogurt and blend well, thinning the mixture with a little milk, if necessary. Season to taste with the hot sauce.

Fill the avocado shells with the soup and top each with a generous dab of sour cream, and caviar, if desired.

Serves 6

CHILLED CUCUMBER SOUP

Fast to make and low in calories, this is an all-time favorite. Use "burpless" or "English" cucumbers for this recipe. If using another variety, be sure to remove the seeds and center pulp completely before using.

2   large or 3 small cucumbers, peeled, seeded, and cut
      into chunks
2   scallions, including tops, trimmed and coarsely chopped
1   garlic clove, peeled
1   cup plain yogurt
4   tablespoons fresh dill
    Salt and freshly ground pepper to taste

Place all the ingredients in a food processor or blender and process until smooth. Chill well before serving.

Serves 4

CURRIED ZUCCHINI SOUP

This soup is good served hot or cold. Depending on your taste, use either a hot Indian-style curry powder or the milder Jamaican variety.

2   cups chicken broth, homemade (see page 25) or canned
6   medium zucchini, ends removed, cut into 2-inch chunks
1   medium onion, coarsely chopped
1   tablespoon curry powder, or to taste
¾   cup light cream

Place the broth in a medium saucepan, add the zucchini and onion, and simmer over low heat until the vegetables are tender, 10 to 15 minutes. Remove from the heat and cool slightly.

Working in batches, remove the vegetables to a food processor or blender and process until smooth. Return to the broth and whisk in the curry powder and cream until well blended. Serve chilled or warm, according to taste.

Serves 6

EASY GAZPACHO

The star of summer soups, this liquid salad is a great way to use up excess produce from the garden. Gazpacho freezes extraordinarily well, so make a big batch and store some away for a breath of summer sometime in February. Though my instructions call for only a couple of whirls in the blender, some gazpacho buffs prefer to purée half of the vegetables, then finely chop the other half to add texture to the soup. Either way—the results are wonderful!

1 bunch scallions (about 6), including tops, trimmed and coarsely chopped

3 garlic cloves, peeled

2 large green bell peppers, seeded and cut into chunks

2 medium cucumbers, peeled and seeded

3 large tomatoes, peeled and seeded plus 4 cups tomato juice, or 6 large tomatoes, peeled and seeded plus 1 tablespoon tomato paste

¼ cup extra-virgin olive oil

2 tablespoons balsamic vinegar

Salt and freshly ground pepper to taste

1 tablespoon hot salsa (optional)

Place all of the ingredients in a food processor or blender. Working in batches, if necessary, purée until smooth. Chill thoroughly. To serve, pour into chilled mugs over a couple of ice cubes.

Serves 6 to 8

COLD DILL AND SHRIMP SOUP

If you're really in a hurry, substitute two to three 6-ounce cans of tiny shrimp, drained, for the cooked shrimp.

1 generous teaspoon Dijon-style mustard
1 quart buttermilk
3 celery stalks, finely chopped
6 radishes, ends removed, thinly sliced
4 scallions, including tops, trimmed and finely chopped
1 pound shrimp, cooked, peeled, and coarsely chopped
¼ cup chopped fresh dill, or more to taste

Combine all the ingredients in a large bowl, cover, and chill 4 to 6 hours.
   Serves 4 to 6

GREEN SUMMER SOUP

Ideal for those with a bountiful garden, this soup is the perfect way to use up an overabundance of summer vegetables.

  4 cups chicken stock, homemade (see page 25) or canned
1½ cups chopped green beans
  ½ cup chopped zucchini
  ½ cup chopped romaine lettuce
  ½ cup fresh peas or chopped sugar snap peas
  ¾ cup chopped celery, with leaves
  ½ cup chopped scallions
  ¼ cup chopped fresh basil
     Salt and freshly ground pepper to taste
  ¼ cup chopped fresh parsley, for garnish

In a large saucepan, combine all of the ingredients except the salt and pepper and parsley. Bring to a boil, reduce the heat, and simmer until the vegetables are tender, 15 to 20 minutes.

Working in batches, purée the vegetables until smooth. Season to taste with salt and pepper. Chill thoroughly and garnish with chopped parsley.

Serves 6

SUMMER SUNSET SOUP

So named because of its surprising pink color, which frankly isn't even close to a sunset pink. Nevertheless, this is one of the simplest soups ever invented. All you need is a liking for beets and a blender.

    2 jars (16 ounces each) pickled beets, drained of half the juice
    2 cups sour cream (reserving 1 to 2 tablespoons, for garnish)
       Fresh parsley (optional)

Place the beets, reserved juice, and sour cream in a food processor or blender and process until very smooth. Chill thoroughly. Before serving, garnish each portion with a dab of sour cream and a sprig of fresh parsley, if desired.

Serves 4

MIXED BERRY SOUP

A cool and light soup, perfect for beautiful summertime berries. When using raspberries in this recipe, you may want to strain the fruit purée to remove the seeds.

> 3 cups mixed berries—raspberries, strawberries, blueberries, or blackberries
> 1 cup vanilla yogurt
> 1 cup orange juice
> ¼ cup rosé or zinfandel wine
> 2 tablespoons confectioners' sugar
> 1 teaspoon grated orange zest

Purée the berries in a food processor or blender. Strain as desired to remove seeds.

Combine the purée with the remaining ingredients and mix until well blended and smooth. Cover and chill thoroughly.

Serves 4 to 6

COLD STRAWBERRY SOUP

Ever have a summer lunch roll around and want nothing more than a huge, drippy bowl of ice cream? Try this wonderful soup instead. It's sweetly satisfying and much lower in fat and calories than Rocky Road.

1 pint strawberries, washed and hulled
2 cups buttermilk
⅓ cup sugar
⅓ cup sour cream, nonfat sour cream, or plain yogurt
4 tablespoons kirsch, or other strawberry-flavored liqueur

Place all the ingredients in a food processor or blender. Process until smooth. Serve well chilled.

Serves 4

KIWI SOUP
....

Somewhere between strawberry and melon, the distinct flavor of the tropical kiwifruit is unsurpassed. Do experiment with other delicately flavored juices in place of the apple juice, such as some of the popular apple-raspberry or apple-strawberry combinations, for different effects.

10 kiwis, peeled and cubed, about 3 cups
1 cup apple juice
1 cup vanilla yogurt, or 1 cup low-fat sour cream combined
   with 1 teaspoon vanilla extract
2 tablespoons confectioners' sugar

Purée the fruit in a food processor or blender. Remove to a bowl and combine with the remaining ingredients until smooth. Chill.

Serves 4 to 6

MELON MADNESS

My favorite thing about this soup is the pale, creamy orange color. Irresistible! Remember, when buying melons, test for ripeness by smelling them. Turn to the stem end and sniff. The stronger the smell, the riper the melon. Much more reliable than thumping.

2 cups cubed cantaloupe
2 cups cubed honeydew melon
1/4 cup orange juice
1 cup low-fat or nonfat sour cream
2 tablespoons confectioners' sugar
Fresh mint, for garnish (optional)

Combine all the ingredients except the mint. Working in batches, if necessary, purée in a food processor or blender until smooth.

Chill thoroughly, ladle into individual bowls or mugs, and garnish with fresh mint, if desired.

Serves 6

CREAM OF MANGO SOUP

Be sure of the freshness of your eggs when you make this soup, though a good shot of rum goes a long way toward killing any germs.

2 eggs
3 tablespoons dark rum
⅓ cup sugar
   Juice and grated zest of 1 large lemon
1 large mango, peeled, pitted, and cut into chunks
4 cups half-and-half or light cream
   Fresh berries, for garnish (optional)

In a blender or food processor, purée the eggs with the rum, sugar, and lemon juice and zest until very light.

Add the mango chunks and process until smooth. Slowly add the half-and-half or light cream; blend well. Chill thoroughly and garnish with fresh berries, if desired.

Serves 4

Bread and Tomato Soup

Champagne Chicken Soup

Grandma's Chicken Soup • Yogurt Soup

Cabbage-Barley Soup • Carrot-Orange Soup

Beet Hater's Borscht • Sopa de Lima (Lime Soup)

Tortilla Soup • Cajun Potato Soup • Easy Onion Soup

Cider Soup • Spinach and Dandelion Soup

Stracciatella • Goober Soup • Walnut Soup

Chestnut Soup • Garlic Soup • Sausage Soup

Beer Soup • Filipino Corn Soup

Italian Wedding Soup • Shaker Soup

Moroccan Lamb Soup

Hot and Satisfying Soups

These four words say it all when it comes to describing the irresistible soups that can be made with a minimum of time, effort, and expense. Most of the recipes here are a meal in themselves, and any leftovers can be frozen in individual portions and microwaved for a fast lunch or snack. Do let the recipes here be your inspiration rather than your bible, however. While all of them are tested and true, there is nothing like a potful of soup to bring out your culinary genius. A handful of this, a sprinkle of that, and before you know it you'll have created something all your own!

BREAD AND TOMATO SOUP

In a soup this simple, the secret of success is in the individual ingredients. Use only the finest extra-virgin olive oil and a good coarse-textured semolina or other peasant-type bread. You won't be disappointed!

- ¾ cup extra-virgin olive oil
- 4 large garlic cloves, peeled and diced
- ½ cup fresh sage leaves
- ½ pound stale coarse-textured bread, thinly sliced
- 1 can (22 ounces) tomatoes, undrained and lightly chopped, or 4 large fresh tomatoes, peeled and diced
- 8 cups beef broth, homemade (see page 25) or canned
  Salt and freshly ground pepper to taste

Place the oil and diced garlic in a wide-bottomed saucepan and sauté over high heat until the garlic begins to color. Add the sage leaves and continue cooking until the oil is quite hot, but not burning.

Add the bread slices to the oil, a few at a time, browning on both sides. Add the tomatoes with their juice and the broth, cover, and simmer for 20 minutes. Season with salt and pepper to taste.

Serves 6

CHAMPAGNE CHICKEN SOUP

One of the great things about soup is that it is so economical to make, as evidenced by the following recipe, concocted almost entirely of dinner-party leftovers. Note the use of gravy as a soup base—a terrific, thrifty substitute for the usual stock.

    1   **cup diced cooked chicken**
    1   **cup leftover chicken gravy, prepared gravy mix, or canned chicken gravy**
    2   **cups water**
$1\frac{1}{2}$ **cups champagne or still white wine**
    1   **onion, finely chopped**
    2   **garlic cloves, peeled and pressed**
    1   **carrot, scrubbed and diced**
    2   **celery stalks with leaves, diced**
    1   **teaspoon poultry seasoning**
 $\frac{1}{2}$ **cup white rice**

In a medium saucepan, combine the chicken, gravy, water, and champagne or wine. Place over medium heat and add the vegetables and seasoning. Simmer until the vegetables are tender.

Add the rice, bring to a boil, and reduce the heat. Cover and simmer 15 to 20 minutes, or until the rice is tender and the soup is thickened.

Serves 4

GRANDMA'S CHICKEN SOUP

Is it really a cure-all? Who knows? My own feeling is, anything that tastes this good is bound to make you feel better. According to Grandma, fresh dill is the secret!

4   cups chicken broth, homemade (see page 25) or canned
1   pound chicken parts, or 1 cup diced cooked chicken
2   garlic cloves, peeled and pressed
1   large onion, coarsely chopped
2   celery stalks with leaves, diced
1   package (10 ounces) frozen peas and carrots
1   bay leaf
    Salt and pepper to taste
¼   cup chopped fresh dill

Place all of the ingredients together in a large saucepan. Cover and simmer over medium heat for 20 minutes (add 10 to 15 minutes if using uncooked chicken), or until the vegetables are tender.

If using uncooked chicken, remove the chicken from the saucepan and allow to cool slightly. Discard the skin and bones, dice the remaining meat, and return to the soup. Heat thoroughly before serving.

Serves 6

Yogurt Soup

This soup is a lovely color and its creamy texture makes for an exciting contrast with the bite of the spices. Equally good with chicken or shrimp, it's necessary to stabilize the yogurt with cornstarch before cooking, so that it won't curdle.

1½ cups plain yogurt
¼ cup cornstarch
¼ cup cold water
8 cups chicken or fish stock, homemade (see page 25) or canned
1 small onion, minced
¼ teaspoon cayenne pepper to taste
1 teaspoon paprika to taste
   Salt and freshly ground pepper to taste
1 cup diced cooked chicken, or ⅓ pound shrimp, peeled, deveined, and diced
1 large egg, beaten

In a large saucepan, combine the yogurt, cornstarch, and water. Whisk lightly until well blended. Place over low heat and simmer, stirring constantly in one direction only, for 5 to 8 minutes, or until the mixture is thickened and has lost any starchy flavor.

Add the stock, onion, cayenne pepper, paprika, and salt and pepper to the mixture, and blend well. Cook over medium heat, stirring frequently, until creamy. Add the chicken or the shrimp and continue cooking, stirring constantly, until the chicken is heated through or until the shrimp turns pink.

Reduce heat to low. Gradually add several spoonfuls of the hot soup to the beaten egg. Return the egg to the soup, spoonful by spoonful, beating after every addition. Do not allow the soup to boil. Stir constantly until the soup is thickened.

Serves 6

Cabbage-Barley Soup

A fast and easy version of an Old World favorite. Good old ketchup takes the place of a more complicated list of ingredients here, resulting in a sweet-and-sour flavor that never reveals the shortcuts in preparation.

 6 cups beef broth, homemade (see page 25) or canned
 2 cups shredded cabbage
 1 large onion, coarsely chopped
 1 garlic clove, peeled and pressed
 ½ cup barley
 ½ cup ketchup

Combine all of the ingredients in a large saucepan. Bring to a boil over medium heat, cover, and simmer until the barley is tender, about 20 to 25 minutes.

Serves 6

CARROT-ORANGE SOUP

One of my favorites as a starter for holiday dinners, or all by itself for a light and satisfying lunch.

2	cups chicken stock, homemade (see page 25) or canned
4	large carrots, unpeeled and scrubbed, cut into chunks
1	small onion, diced
½	cup orange juice
2	tablespoons freshly grated orange zest
½	cup heavy cream

Place the stock in a medium saucepan, add the carrots and onion, and cook over low heat until the vegetables are tender.

Remove the vegetables to a food processor or blender, reserving the stock, and process until puréed.

Mix the purée, orange juice, and zest into the stock. Cook over medium heat until steaming, stirring occasionally. Add the cream and stir to blend. Continue to cook just until heated through.

Serves 4

BEET HATER'S BORSCHT

Tom Robbins once said that beets are the most serious of all vegetables. It is true that beets provoke serious reactions—you either love them or you hate them. Nevertheless, even the most dedicated beet haters will be converted by this delicious soup. The beets take a backseat to the sweet-and-sour tang of the soup itself, and the other vegetables see to it that this doesn't taste only of beets. To save time and effort, the vegetables can be diced in a food processor, but be careful not to overprocess them. Part of the appeal of this soup is its chunky texture.

1 onion, coarsely chopped

1 carrot, scrubbed and diced

4 medium beets, trimmed, peeled, and finely chopped

1 can (22 ounces) tomatoes, undrained

4 medium potatoes, well scrubbed and cut into small chunks

4 cups shredded cabbage

4 cups chicken, beef, or vegetable stock, homemade (see
      page 25) or canned

3 tablespoons sugar

3 tablespoons cider vinegar

1 tablespoon chopped fresh dill

   Salt and freshly ground pepper to taste

1 cup sour cream, for garnish

Place the vegetables and the stock in a large saucepan and bring to a boil over medium heat. Reduce the heat slightly, cover, and cook until the vegetables are very tender, approximately 30 to 40 minutes.

Add the sugar and vinegar and cook 3 minutes more, or until the vinegar loses it sharpness. Add the dill, and season to taste with salt and pepper. Ladle into bowls and top with generous dollops of sour cream.

Serves 6 to 8

SOPA DE LIMA (LIME SOUP)

Is this easy or what? Lie: say it took hours.

- 2 cups chicken broth, homemade (see page 25) or canned
- 1 cup diced cooked chicken breast
- ½ cup freshly squeezed lime juice
- 1 teaspoon grated lime zest
- 1 teaspoon fresh thyme leaves, or ½ teaspoon dried
  Salt and freshly ground pepper to taste
- 1 bag (12 ounces) tortilla chips

In a medium saucepan, over medium heat, combine the chicken broth with the diced chicken, lime juice, zest, thyme, and salt and pepper to taste. Serve in deep bowls over broken tortilla chips.

Serves 4

TORTILLA SOUP

Fast, easy, and light, this soup is a spicy twist on tomato soup.

1 can (8 ounces) tomatoes, undrained
1 medium onion, diced
1 large clove garlic, peeled
2 tablespoons snipped cilantro
½ teaspoon sugar
4 cups chicken broth, homemade (see page 25) or canned
1 bag (12 ounces) tortilla chips
1 cup shredded jalapeño jack cheese

Place the tomatoes, onion, garlic, cilantro, and sugar in the workbowl of a food processor or blender and process until nearly smooth.

Remove the mixture to a large saucepan and stir in the chicken broth to blend. Bring to a boil, cover, reduce the heat, and simmer for 15 minutes.

Lightly crush the tortilla chips and place in the bottoms of deep bowls. Top with the shredded cheese. Ladle the soup over the chips and cheese and serve immediately.

Serves 6

Cajun Potato Soup

Hearty it is, and wonderfully good. I like to use tiny new red potatoes for this soup.

½ cup vegetable oil
½ cup all-purpose flour
1 large onion, coarsely chopped
½ cup coarsely chopped celery
2 generous teaspoons paprika
1 pound smoked kielbasa sausage, cut into rounds
2 pounds tiny new potatoes, well scrubbed
4 cups hot water
2 garlic cloves, peeled and pressed
½ teaspoon dried thyme
  Salt and freshly ground pepper to taste
1 cup sour cream
  Hot red pepper sauce (optional)

Place the oil and flour in a large saucepan and cook over medium heat, stirring constantly, until golden brown, about 4 minutes.

Add the onion, celery, and paprika and cook until the vegetables are wilted. Add the sausage and potatoes and brown, about 5 minutes.

Add the water, garlic, thyme, and salt and pepper to taste. Simmer until the potatoes are very tender. Stir in the sour cream and continue cooking just until heated through. Season with red pepper sauce, if desired.

Serves 6 to 8

Easy Onion Soup

Nothing to it, really. The trick is to sauté the onions very slowly. Slow-cooking the onions gives them an almost sweet flavor that makes this favorite soup hard to distinguish from the labor-intensive French original.

2 large yellow onions, cut in halves, and sliced very thin
¼ cup (½ stick) unsalted butter, or extra-virgin olive oil
1 can (13¾ ounces) beef broth
1 can (13¾ ounces) chicken broth
1 can water
  Salt and freshly ground pepper to taste
6 slices French bread, toasted until golden brown
6 thick slices Gruyère, raclette, or other good melting cheese

Place the onions and the butter or oil in a large saucepan. Cook, covered, over low heat until the onions are translucent and very limp. Add the broths, water, and salt and pepper to taste. Bring to a boil over medium heat, and continue boiling for 2 to 3 minutes.

Preheat the broiler. Place the soup in ovenproof bowls, top each bowl with a slice of toasted bread and a slice of cheese. Place the bowls on a baking sheet and run under the broiler for 3 to 4 minutes, or until the cheese is melted and bubbly.

Serves 6

CIDER SOUP

Not sweet, not cold—totally unexpected, and utterly irresistible for the first chilly nights in autumn. Note that the vegetables may be minced in the food processor first, to save time and energy.

- 1 cup (2 sticks) unsalted butter
- 1 leek, white part only, washed and minced
- 1 celery stalk, with leaves, finely chopped
- ½ green bell pepper, seeded and minced
- 3 tablespoons all-purpose flour
- ¼ teaspoon dry mustard
- 1 generous dash Worcestershire sauce
- 1 can (13¾ ounces) chicken broth
- 1½ cups grated cheddar cheese
- 1 cup hard apple cider, or ¾ cup apple cider plus ¼ cup apple brandy
- ½ cup heavy cream
- Salt and freshly ground pepper to taste
- Fresh parsley, for garnish (optional)

In a large saucepan, melt the butter until foaming. Add the vegetables and sauté over medium heat until limp but not browned, about 3 minutes. Add the flour, mustard, and Worcestershire sauce and continue cooking, stirring well, until the flour begins to stick, about 2 to 3 minutes.

Add the broth and bring to a boil. Add the grated cheese and heat, stirring constantly, until the cheese melts completely, about 2 minutes.

Stir in the cider and cream and continue cooking just until the mixture is heated through—do not allow it to boil. Season with salt and pepper to taste. Ladle into bowls or mugs and garnish with fresh parsley, if desired.

Serves 6

SPINACH AND DANDELION SOUP

Dandelion greens are increasingly available in supermarkets and produce stores, but if you do pick your own, opt for the young, fresh variety with no fuzz.

- 6 cups chicken or vegetable stock, homemade (see page 25) or canned
- 3 cups coarsely chopped fresh dandelion greens
- 3 cups coarsely chopped fresh spinach
- 2 garlic cloves, peeled and pressed
- 1 small sweet red or Vidalia onion, peeled and sliced paper thin
- $\frac{1}{2}$ teaspoon ground nutmeg

Salt and freshly ground pepper to taste

- 2 hard-boiled eggs, peeled and finely chopped, for garnish

In a large saucepan, combine all of the ingredients except the eggs. Bring to a boil over medium heat. Reduce the heat and simmer until the greens are tender, about 15 minutes. Ladle the soup into bowls and garnish with chopped eggs.

Serves 6

STRACCIATELLA

This delicate Roman specialty is a natural for brunch or for trying to sneak some protein into finicky kids. The hot broth effectively cooks the eggs as they are swirled through the soup.

  3 cups chicken broth, homemade (see page 25) or canned
  3 large eggs
  ¼ cup fresh bread crumbs
  ¼ cup grated Parmesan cheese
  ¼ teaspoon ground nutmeg

In a medium saucepan, bring the broth to a boil over medium heat. Meanwhile, lightly beat the eggs, bread crumbs, cheese, and nutmeg together in a small bowl. Remove the broth from the heat long enough to pour in the egg mixture. Return the soup to a boil, stirring constantly with a whisk.

Serves 6

GOOBER SOUP

For peanut lovers everywhere, Goober Soup makes wonderful use of ingredients that most likely you have on hand.

  1   cup (2 sticks) unsalted butter
  1   small green bell pepper, coarsely chopped
  2   celery stalks with leaves, diced
  1   large onion, coarsely chopped
  3   tablespoons all-purpose flour
  4   cups chicken broth, homemade (see page 25) or canned
  1   cup chunky peanut butter
 ½   teaspoon onion salt
 ½   teaspoon garlic salt
  1   teaspoon paprika
 ½   teaspoon dried thyme
  1   cup light cream or evaporated milk
 ½   cup finely chopped scallions, for garnish
 ½   cup roasted salted peanuts, for garnish

In a large saucepan, heat the butter until foaming. Add the vegetables and cook over medium heat, stirring occasionally, until limp.

Remove the vegetables to a food processor or blender and purée until smooth. Return to the saucepan and stir in the flour. Stir in the broth and cook over low heat until the mixture is slightly thickened.

Add the peanut butter and spices, stirring until well blended. Reduce the heat to low, add the cream or evaporated milk, and heat through, but do not allow to boil. Garnish individual servings with chopped scallions and roasted peanuts.

Serves 6

WALNUT SOUP

A truly unique soup that owes its special flavor to the rich walnuts. Try it with some good bread and a great salad for a light meal.

    ¾ cup walnuts, broken into pieces
    2 large garlic cloves, peeled
  1¾ cups chicken broth, homemade (see page 25) or canned
    2 cups light cream
       Salt and freshly ground pepper to taste

Place the walnuts and garlic in a food processor or blender with 2 or 3 tablespoons of the broth. Process 1 to 2 minutes or until the mixture forms a paste.

Remove the paste to a medium-size saucepan and whisk in the remaining broth, a little at a time, until the mixture is smooth. Bring to a boil over medium heat. Add the cream and continue cooking, stirring constantly, until the soup is heated through. Do not allow it to boil. Season to taste with salt and pepper.

Serves 4

CHESTNUT SOUP

As easy as this marvelous soup is to prepare, it has a wonderful, earthy, exotic flavor that guests may find hard to identify.

1	pound chestnuts
2	large onions, diced
3	tablespoons unsalted butter
	Salt and freshly ground pepper to taste
1	cup chicken stock, homemade (see page 25) or canned
1	cup milk
½	cup heavy cream
¼	cup sherry or bourbon

Slit the tops of the chestnuts with a sharp knife. Place them in a large kettle with water to cover. Bring to a boil over medium heat and cook for 20 to 30 minutes, or until soft, but not mushy. Drain and set aside to cool. Peel the chestnuts, removing both the inner and outer skins.

Sauté the onions in the butter over medium-high heat until they are translucent. Add the chestnuts and season with salt and pepper to taste.

Transfer the mixture to a food processor or blender. Add the chicken stock and the milk and purée until smooth. Return to the saucepan and heat just to the boiling point. Stir in the cream and the sherry or bourbon and heat again, but do not allow the mixture to boil.

Serves 6

GARLIC SOUP

The French believe that garlic soup, like chicken soup, is good for what ails you, and there is evidence that garlic cleanses the blood and kills certain kinds of germs in the system. While the most basic version of this soup is made with plain water, I use homemade chicken broth. That way, all bases are covered! This soup is best served with sliced French bread or croutons.

> 4 cups chicken broth, homemade (see page 25)
> 2 heads garlic, cloves separated and peeled
> ½ cup white wine
> ½ cup soup pasta (orzo, pastina, etc., or thin spaghetti broken into tiny pieces)
> 1 fresh tomato, peeled and chopped, or ½ cup chopped canned tomatoes
> ½ teaspoon ground thyme

In a medium saucepan over medium heat, bring the broth to a boil, and add the garlic cloves. Reduce the heat, cover, and simmer for 20 minutes, or until the garlic is tender.

Add the wine, pasta, tomato, and thyme and continue cooking over low heat, stirring occasionally, until the pasta is done, about 20 minutes. Serve the soup very hot.

Serves 4

SAUSAGE SOUP

An Italian dinner in a bowl. Serve with a loaf of crusty garlic bread and a rough red wine. This recipe makes quite a lot, but can be halved successfully, or made in one batch and frozen in smaller portions for later use.

1½ pounds Italian sausage, hot or sweet
  3 garlic cloves, peeled and pressed
  2 large onions, coarsely chopped
  1 green bell pepper, seeded and coarsely chopped
  1 can (22 ounces) Italian-style tomatoes, undrained
  5 cups beef broth, homemade (see page 25) or 3 cans (13¾ ounces each)
½ teaspoon fennel seed
½ teaspoon dried oregano
  3 tablespoons chopped fresh basil, or 2 teaspoons dried
  3 tablespoons chopped fresh parsley, or 2 teaspoons dried
  2 medium zucchini, cut into fine strips
  5 ounces uncooked pasta (such as bow ties, elbows, or small shells)
    Grated Romano cheese

Cut the sausage into bite-size chunks, and brown in a large saucepan. Drain all but 2 tablespoons of the fat. Add the garlic, onions, and green pepper to the pan and cook until the vegetables are limp.

Add the tomatoes, crushing them lightly with the back of a spoon or fork. Add their juice, the broth, and the seasonings and herbs. Cover and simmer over low heat for 15 minutes.

Add the zucchini and the pasta. Continue cooking over low heat, stirring occasionally, until the pasta is al dente, 10 to 20 minutes, depending on the type of pasta used. Top with the grated cheese.

Serves 6 to 8

Beer Soup

Easy, unusual, and wonderfully good! Though I've suggested an extra-sharp cheddar, any strongly flavored cheese or combination of cheeses will do.

  1   **green bell pepper, seeded and minced**
  1   **bunch scallions (6 to 8), including tops, trimmed and finely chopped**
  2   **tablespoons bacon fat or extra-virgin olive oil**
  2   **cups instant mashed potato flakes (see Note)**
1½ **cups water**
16 **ounces good dark beer, stout, or ale, at room temperature**
1¼ **cups grated extra-sharp cheddar cheese**
  1   **tablespoon Dijon-style mustard**

In a medium saucepan, sauté the green pepper and scallions in the bacon fat or olive oil over medium heat until limp and lightly browned. Add the potato flakes and water, blending with a fork until the mixture is free of lumps. Add the beer, blend, and continue cooking for 3 minutes.

Reduce the heat to low and add the cheese a little at a time, whisking constantly until the cheese is melted and the soup is smooth. Stir in the mustard and serve.

Serves 6

NOTE: Follow package directions for the amount of water necessary to reconstitute the potato flakes, or thin the soup with a little milk, if required.

FILIPINO CORN SOUP

A fabulous combination of corn and shrimp. Use fresh corn cut off the cob or drained canned corn.

2 tablespoons extra-virgin olive oil
1 large, sweet red or Vidalia onion, sliced paper thin
2 garlic cloves, peeled and pressed
½ pound uncooked small or medium shrimp, peeled, deveined, and diced
2 cups bottled clam juice
1½ cups water
1½ cups corn kernels
½ cup shredded spinach fresh or frozen, thawed, and drained
Salt and freshly ground pepper to taste

Place the oil in a medium saucepan. Add the onion and garlic and sauté over medium heat until they are limp. Add the shrimp and continue to sauté just until they turn pink, about 2 minutes.

Add the clam juice, water, and corn. Reduce the heat and simmer for 10 minutes. Add the spinach and continue cooking an additional 2 or 3 minutes. Season to taste with salt and pepper.

Serves 6

ITALIAN WEDDING SOUP

This one's so easy, it's almost ridiculous. Serve as a meal when you want to impress without spending much time or effort.

    ½   pound ground beef
    1   large egg
    ¾   cup Italian-flavored bread crumbs
    1   teaspoon salt
    2   teaspoons freshly ground black pepper
    2   cups chicken broth, homemade (see page 25) or canned
    1   package (12 ounces) chopped frozen spinach

Preheat the oven to 400° F.

Combine the beef, egg, bread crumbs, salt, and pepper. Form into tiny meatballs about the size of a marble and place on an ungreased baking sheet. Bake for 10 minutes, or until firm.

Meanwhile, bring the broth and spinach to a boil in a large saucepan over medium heat. Reduce the heat, add the meatballs, and simmer gently for 20 minutes.

Serves 6

SHAKER SOUP

Like the famed Shaker furniture designs, this soup is simplicity itself, but with an indefinable elegance.

1	tablespoon unsalted butter
3	tablespoons minced fresh chives
3	tablespoons minced fresh chervil
1	tablespoon minced fresh lovage or celery leaves
3	tablespoons minced fresh sorrel
2	tablespoons minced fresh summer savory
1	teaspoon minced fresh tarragon
3	stalks celery, finely chopped
4	cups chicken broth, homemade (see page 25) or canned
	Salt and freshly ground pepper to taste
6	slices coarse-textured bread, toasted
½	teaspoon ground nutmeg
1	cup grated cheddar or Muenster cheese

Melt the butter in a medium saucepan until foaming. Add the chopped fresh herbs and celery and sauté over medium heat for 3 minutes.

Add the broth and salt and pepper to taste. Simmer gently for 15 minutes to allow the flavors to blend.

Place the toast slices in individual serving bowls or a soup tureen. Pour the soup over the toast. Sprinkle with the nutmeg and top with cheese.

Serves 6

MOROCCAN LAMB SOUP

For hearty appetites, this soup is traditionally served over couscous, a semolina that can be likened to a fine pasta or grits, depending on your part of the world. Note the unusual combination of ingredients here, unique to this region of North Africa. Delicious!

2   tablespoons extra-virgin olive oil
1   pound lamb, cubed
1   quart water
1   teaspoon salt
4   carrots, scrubbed, ends removed, and diced
2   onions, chopped
2   tablespoons tomato paste
$\frac{1}{2}$ teaspoon saffron threads
$\frac{1}{4}$ teaspoon ground ginger
$\frac{1}{4}$ teaspoon allspice
$\frac{1}{3}$ cup raisins
1   cup chopped zucchini
1   cup canned chick-peas, drained
2   large tomatoes, chopped, or 1 can (8 ounces) tomatoes
3   tablespoons chopped fresh parsley
   Hot red pepper sauce to taste

In a large saucepan, heat the olive oil and fry the cubed lamb until well-browned. Add the water, salt, carrots, onions, and tomato paste. Reduce the heat; cover and simmer until the lamb is very tender, approximately 40 minutes.

Add the spices, raisins, zucchini, chick-peas, and tomatoes, and simmer for an additional 20 minutes. Just before serving, stir in the chopped fresh parsley and add red pepper sauce to taste.

Serves 6 to 8

Bean with Bacon Soup • Cuban Black Bean Soup

Tomato and Bean Soup • Black-eyed Bonanza

Hummus Soup • Spinach and Red Lentil Soup

Bean and Broccoli Rabe Soup

BOUNTIFUL BEAN SOUPS

In these health-conscious times, people are rapidly rediscovering the bountiful bean as a source of protein, fiber, and all-around nourishment. Always keep some beans on hand in the cupboard or pantry. They're cheap, chock-full of all the good stuff, and a wonderful addition to all kinds of meals, not just soup. Either dried or canned beans can be used in any of the recipes that follow, but keep in mind that dried beans require a longer preparation time. Follow package directions for presoaking dried beans, and remember, to degas beans, discard the soaking liquid—that's where the troublemaking enzymes reside. On the other hand, when adding canned beans to soup, don't drain them. The canning liquid helps to thicken the soup.

Bean with Bacon Soup

A must for bean soup lovers. Depending on how much time you have, you may easily substitute precooked mixed dried beans for the canned beans called for in this recipe.

½ pound bacon, diced
1 large onion, diced
2 carrots, scrubbed and diced
1 green bell pepper, seeded and diced
2 garlic cloves, peeled and pressed
3 cups water
1 can (8 ounces) tomato sauce
2 cans (16 ounces each) any variety of beans, such as black, pink, kidney, or garbanzo, undrained
Hot sauce to taste

Place the bacon in a large saucepan and fry over medium heat until crisp and browned. Remove from the pan and set aside, reserving 3 tablespoons of the fat.

Sauté the onion, carrots, green pepper, and garlic in the reserved bacon fat until limp. Carefully add the water, tomato sauce, and beans. Simmer over medium heat, stirring occasionally, for 15 to 20 minutes, or until the mixture is slightly thickened. Add the reserved bacon bits and season with hot sauce to taste.

Serves 6 to 8

CUBAN BLACK BEAN SOUP

A shortcut version of a real classic. Cuban-style beans are available in the ethnic or gourmet section of most grocery stores.

2   **cups beef, ham, or vegetable stock, homemade (see page 25) or canned**
1   **cup water**
1   **medium onion, diced**
2   **garlic cloves, peeled and pressed**
2   **celery stalks, with leaves, finely chopped**
2   **carrots, scrubbed and finely chopped**
2   **cans (16 ounces each) Cuban-style black beans, undrained**
1   **generous teaspoon cumin**
    Salt and freshly ground pepper to taste
¼   **cup sherry**

Place all the ingredients except the seasonings and sherry in a large saucepan over medium heat. Reduce the heat, cover, and simmer 20 to 30 minutes, or until the vegetables are tender.

Strain the soup and return the broth to the saucepan. Working in batches, purée the beans and vegetables in a food processor or blender.

Combine the purée with the broth until smooth. Add the cumin and salt and pepper to taste. Heat thoroughly, stirring occasionally. Just before serving, stir in the sherry.

Serves 6 to 8

TOMATO AND BEAN SOUP

Fast and easy, this soup will stick to your ribs for much longer than the time it took to make it.

1   can (16 ounces) stewed tomatoes, undrained
1   can (16 ounces) any variety beans in tomato sauce
1   cup water
3   scallions, including tops, trimmed and finely chopped
½   teaspoon cumin
1   tablespoon chopped fresh parsley
     Generous dash of hot sauce, or to taste
½   cup shredded cheddar cheese

Combine all of the ingredients except the cheese in a medium saucepan. Bring to a boil, then reduce the heat and simmer for 10 minutes, stirring occasionally. Ladle into bowls and sprinkle with cheese.

Serves 4 to 6

BLACK-EYED BONANZA

People throughout the southern United States eat black-eyed peas on New Year's Eve or New Year's Day to bring good luck in the coming year. This soup is an excellent choice for a New Year's brunch or supper. The extra bite of hot sauce is good for those New Year's hangovers, too.

½ pound bacon, diced
3 carrots, scrubbed and diced
3 medium onions, coarsely chopped
2 cups diced celery
1 meaty ham bone, or 2 pounds smoked pork hocks
8 cups water
2 cans (16 ounces each) black-eyed peas, undrained
2 to 3 teaspoons hot red pepper sauce, or to taste
3 bay leaves
½ teaspoon dried thyme

Place the bacon, carrots, onions, and celery in a large saucepan and cook over medium heat until the onions are golden, about 8 minutes.

Add the remaining ingredients, cover, and simmer over low heat for 25 to 30 minutes. Remove and discard the bay leaves. Remove the ham bone or hocks from the soup, cut any meat from the bones, and dice. Return to the soup.

Serves 8 to 10

HUMMUS SOUP

This is an easy version of a classic Lebanese soup—perfect for vegetarians. Serve this soup with toasted pita bread on the side.

  2   **cans (16 ounces each) chick-peas, undrained**
1½ **quarts water, or vegetable stock, homemade**
      (see page 25) or canned
  1   **generous teaspoon salt**
  3   **garlic cloves, peeled and pressed**
⅓ **cup extra-virgin olive oil**
  2   **medium onions, thinly sliced**
  2   **tablespoons sesame paste**
      Juice of 2 lemons (about ⅓ cup)

Place the chick-peas, water or stock, salt, garlic, oil, and onions in a large saucepan. Simmer over medium heat until the onions are tender, about 20 minutes.

Add the sesame paste and lemon juice and stir to blend. Remove the mixture to a food processor or blender, and working in batches, process until puréed. Serve hot or chilled.

Serves 6

SPINACH AND RED LENTIL SOUP

This earthy combination of flavors lends itself to a variety of spices and seasonings, or works as is. Red lentils are available in health and ethnic food stores. Some kinds of lentils cook more quickly than others, but do make sure they are tender. Lentils are just not meant to be served al dente.

1   cup red lentils, washed and presoaked according to package directions
8   cups chicken, beef, or vegetable stock, homemade (see page 25) or canned
1   large onion, coarsely chopped
1   teaspoon salt
1   package (10 ounces) frozen spinach, thawed and drained
    Lemon wedges, for garnish

Drain and combine the lentils with the stock, onion, and salt in a large saucepan. Bring to a boil, reduce the heat, cover, and simmer 20 to 30 minutes, or until the lentils are tender. Add the spinach and continue cooking another 5 minutes, or until heated through.

Ladle into bowls and garnish with lemon wedges.

Serves 6

BEAN AND BROCCOLI RABE SOUP

Broccoli rabe and white kidney or cannellini beans make for an unbeatable combination, loaded with nutrients, fiber, and flavor. You may substitute any greens for the broccoli rabe—Swiss chard, kale, and turnip or beet greens all work wonderfully well.

¼ cup extra-virgin olive oil
1 pound broccoli rabe, washed, trimmed, and shredded
4 large garlic cloves, peeled and pressed
1 large red sweet onion, sliced very thin
8 cups chicken or vegetable broth, homemade (see page 25) or canned
1 can (16 ounces) cannellini or white kidney beans, undrained
Grated Parmesan cheese

In a large saucepan, heat the oil slightly over medium heat. Add the broccoli rabe, garlic, and onion. Stir once or twice, cover the pan, and continue cooking 3 to 4 minutes, or until the greens are wilted.

Add the broth and the beans. Bring to a boil, reduce the heat to low, and simmer 10 to 15 minutes, or until the soup is very hot and the greens are tender. Ladle into bowls and top with Parmesan cheese.

Serves 6

Cream of Almond Soup

Cheater's Cream of Chicken and Avocado Soup

Cream of Eggplant Soup

Cream of Leek Soup • Cream of Mushroom Soup

Cream of Broccoli Soup • Plantain Chowder

Corn and Green Chile Chowder

Freshwater Fish Chowder • Cheddar Chowder

Corn Bisque with Chicken or Crabmeat

Salmon Bisque • Mixed Greens Bisque

Oyster Stew • Sea Scallop Soup

CREAMY CLASSICS, CHOWDERS, AND BISQUES

Cream soups, chowders, and bisques are a fabulous and filling choice for any meal. Though you may be inclined to steer away from the higher fat content of cream soups, keep in mind that serving per serving these delights are still relatively low-fat compared to meats and cheeses, and that some creamy soups don't use cream at all, but a healthier choice, like polenta, for thickening. Those who wish to limit fat content even further can substitute evaporated skim milk for light or heavy cream, or experiment even further by skipping the milk or cream altogether, and substituting an equal amount of broth instead. If the soup needs thickening, add flour or cornstarch.

CREAM OF ALMOND SOUP

Garnish this wonder with toasted almonds and pumpkin seeds
for additional dazzle.

3   **cups chicken broth, homemade (see page 25) or canned**
1   **can (16 ounces) pumpkin**
2   **tablespoons unsalted butter**
1   **small yellow onion, coarsely chopped**
1   **celery stalk with leaves, diced**
3   **generous tablespoons almond paste**
1   **tablespoon tomato paste**
$1\frac{1}{3}$ **cups light cream or half-and-half**
$\frac{1}{4}$ **cup almond-flavored liqueur**
    Dash of ground nutmeg
    Salt and freshly ground pepper to taste

Combine the broth and canned pumpkin in a medium saucepan and set aside. Melt the butter in a small sauté pan over low heat. Add the onion and celery and cook until the vegetables are translucent, about 5 minutes.

Add the onion mixture and the almond and tomato pastes to the pumpkin mixture, blending until smooth. Cook over medium heat, stirring occasionally, for 15 minutes. Add the cream or half-and-half and continue cooking until the soup is heated through. Just before serving, add the liqueur and nutmeg, and season to taste with salt and pepper.

Serves 6 to 8

CHEATER'S CREAM OF CHICKEN AND AVOCADO SOUP

Our mothers knew the tricks of using canned cream soups as the basis for all sorts of down-home concoctions. Though I'm not an advocate of overdoing the canned stuff, the following is one of those "haute canned" recipes that can be a godsend when you want a five-minute dinner soup with a lot of flavor and a lot of class.

1   can (13¾ ounces) cream of chicken soup plus 1 can
        cold water
1   tablespoon grated onion
1   canned pimento, cut into fine slivers
½   teaspoon chili powder
½   teaspoon grated lemon peel
½   medium avocado, finely diced

In a medium saucepan, combine all the ingredients. Place over low heat, cover, and simmer for 5 minutes. Remove the cover and stir the soup to blend and soften the avocado pieces slightly.

Serves 4

CREAM OF EGGPLANT SOUP

This makes a thick soup, with an almost indefinable yet very important hint of curry. Try to use small eggplants if possible, or the milder Italian variety. Peel the eggplants completely to avoid any bitterness and to save time, chop the vegetables in a food processor.

$\frac{1}{4}$ cup ($\frac{1}{2}$ stick) unsalted butter
2 medium onions, coarsely chopped
4 celery stalks, coarsely chopped
2 medium potatoes, peeled and finely chopped
3 pounds eggplant, peeled and finely chopped
4 cups chicken, beef, or vegetable stock,
      homemade (see page 25) or canned
1 teaspoon curry powder
$\frac{1}{2}$ teaspoon dried thyme
2 cups heavy cream

In a large saucepan, heat the butter until foaming. Add the vegetables. Cook over medium heat, stirring occasionally, until the ingredients begin to stick to the bottom of the pan, about 15 minutes.

Add the stock and seasonings and continue cooking until the soup begins to thicken, about another 15 minutes. Add the cream and continue cooking until the soup is heated through, but do not allow it to boil.

Serves 6 to 8

CREAM OF LEEK SOUP

Always a delight. The tricky thing about leeks is that they must be washed thoroughly. Soil tends to hide in all those layers, so be careful to spread the leaves apart and hold under running water before dicing. Serve with puff pastry twists instead of bread for an elegant effect.

- 3 cups chicken broth, homemade (see page 25) or canned
- 4 leeks, trimmed, washed, and sliced very thinly, white parts only
- 3 tablespoons unsalted butter, softened
- 2 tablespoons all-purpose flour
- 1⅓ cups light cream or evaporated milk
  Salt and freshly ground pepper to taste

In a medium saucepan, bring the broth to a boil. Add the leeks, reduce the heat, and simmer 10 minutes.

Meanwhile, using your fingertips, knead the butter and flour into a paste. Break it into small pieces.

Add the cream or evaporated milk and bits of the butter paste to the broth and cook, stirring constantly, until the soup is slightly thickened. Season to taste with salt and pepper.

Serves 6

CREAM OF MUSHROOM SOUP

Not to be confused with that pallid stuff your Mom used to dump over the meat-loaf, this version is made with large portobello mushrooms, which have a texture and taste that is closer to steak than mushrooms. As exotic mushrooms are becoming increasingly available all over the country, don't be afraid to experiment with other varieties—shiitake, cremini, and even reconstituted dried porcini or cèpes will make a welcome addition to this marvelous soup.

> 8 ounces portobello mushrooms
> 3 cups chicken or vegetable stock, homemade (see page 25) or canned
> 1½ cups heavy cream
> 2 tablespoons unsweetened chestnut paste
> Salt and freshly ground pepper to taste
> Fresh Italian parsley, for garnish

Clean the mushrooms with a damp cloth, but do not wash them. Cut into julienne strips and set aside.

In a medium saucepan, bring the stock to a boil. Add the mushrooms and simmer over medium heat until tender.

Add the cream, then stir in the chestnut paste until smooth. Heat thoroughly, but do not allow to boil. Season to taste with salt and pepper. Garnish with fresh parsley before serving.

Serves 4 to 6

CREAM OF BROCCOLI SOUP

In my own opinion, the finest of the cream soups. A fabulous choice for a nippy winter's night.

2	cups broccoli florets
3	cups chicken broth, homemade (see page 25) or canned
1	onion, coarsely chopped
1	carrot, scrubbed and diced
2	tablespoons unsalted butter
2	tablespoons all-purpose flour
1⅓	cups light cream or evaporated milk
1	teaspoon fresh thyme leaves, or ½ teaspoon dried
	Salt and freshly ground pepper to taste

In a medium saucepan, cook the broccoli florets in the broth over medium heat, just until tender, about 5 minutes.

Meanwhile, in a small pan, sauté the onion and carrot in the butter over high heat until lightly browned. Add the flour all at once, and cook, stirring constantly, just until the mixture begins to brown, about 2 minutes.

Add to the broth and broccoli and mix well. Add the cream or evaporated milk, stirring constantly, and continue cooking over medium heat until slightly thickened. Add the thyme, and season to taste with salt and pepper.

Serves 6 to 8

PLANTAIN CHOWDER

American cooks are just beginning to discover the fabulous green plantain, which lends a unique flavor to this full-bodied chowder that is somewhere between that of new potatoes and squash. Wonderful! This simple recipe lends itself to experimenting with a variety of ingredients.

- **2   green plantains, peeled and cut into chunks**
- **4   cups chicken stock, homemade (see page 25) or canned**
- **1½   cups any combination of:**
  - **fresh corn or canned, drained**
  - **chopped green or red bell pepper**
  - **chopped fresh or canned tomatoes**
  - **chopped fresh scallions**
  - **crumbled cooked bacon**
  - **diced cooked ham**

In a medium saucepan, over medium heat, cook the plantains in the stock until tender. Remove from heat and, reserving the stock, place the plantains in a food processor or blender. Purée until smooth. Add the purée and the other ingredients to the stock and simmer over very low heat, stirring occasionally, until the vegetables are tender, about 15 minutes.

Serves 5 to 6

CORN AND GREEN CHILE CHOWDER

I have a confession to make: I never peel potatoes—it's too much trouble and besides, the skins are where the vitamins are concentrated. Nonetheless, whether you use a peeled or unpeeled potato in this soup, the result will be memorable. Though it can be made in just about half an hour, to save even more time, pre-bake the potato in your microwave before adding it to the soup.

½	pound bacon, diced
3	tablespoons all-purpose flour
2	cups milk
3	cups chicken stock, homemade (see page 25) or canned
1	large Idaho potato, peeled, if desired, and diced
1	large onion, coarsely chopped
2	carrots, scrubbed and diced
2	celery stalks with leaves, diced
3	cups fresh corn, or 1 can (14 ounces) cream-style corn plus 1 can (6 ounces) regular corn kernels, drained, or 2 packages (10 ounces each) frozen corn
2 or 3	canned green chile peppers, finely minced, or to taste
1	fresh tomato, diced, for garnish (optional)

In a large saucepan, fry the bacon until crisp. Remove from the pan and reserve. Drain and discard all but 3 tablespoons of the fat from the pan.

Combine the flour with the fat and cook over low heat, 2 to 3 minutes, or until very lightly colored. Add the milk and stock and blend well.

Add the potato, onion, carrots, and celery to the stock mixture. Cook over very low heat, stirring occasionally, until the vegetables are tender, approximately 20 minutes. Add the corn and continue to simmer an additional 5 to 10 minutes. Add the chiles to taste.

Just before serving, stir in the crumbled bacon, and garnish with diced tomato, if desired.

Serves 6

FRESHWATER FISH CHOWDER

This very French offering contains three of my favorite ingredients—fish, garlic, and wine. Don't be put off by the amount of garlic in this recipe. Cooking garlic in the peels makes for a mild, almost sweet flavor that is not overwhelming.

3   **pounds mixed freshwater fish, such as perch, catfish, and pike, or your preference**

2   **tablespoons extra-virgin olive oil**

5   **cups full-bodied white wine**

1   **head garlic, separated into cloves, unpeeled**

2   **heaping tablespoons all-purpose flour**

3   **tablespoons unsalted butter, softened**

Rinse the fish in cold water and pat dry. Cut into cubes.

Grease the inside of a large saucepan or covered casserole with the olive oil. Add the fish, wine, and garlic cloves and rapidly bring to a boil over high heat. Ignite the wine, and stand back!

Continue to boil hard until the flame has gone out. Reduce the heat and simmer until the garlic cloves are tender, about 10 minutes. Remove the garlic from the soup with a slotted spoon and set aside to cool.

When the garlic has cooled somewhat, slip the cloves from their skins. Mash the garlic with a fork and combine with the flour and butter, kneading well to make a paste. Whisk the garlic paste back into the soup, a little at a time. Continue to simmer for 15 minutes over very low heat.

Serves 6

CHEDDAR CHOWDER

One of my husband's all-time favorites. Serve this to hearty types with big appetites.

2 cups water
2 cups tiny new red potatoes, scrubbed and unpeeled
¾ cup tiny boiling onions, trimmed
3 tablespoons extra-virgin olive oil
2 tablespoons all-purpose flour
1 tablespoon poultry seasoning
3 cups milk
1½ cups shredded extra-sharp cheddar cheese
1 cup cubed cooked ham
1 tablespoon Dijon-style mustard

Place the water, potatoes, and onions in a large saucepan. Bring to a boil over high heat and cook until potatoes are tender, about 15 minutes.

Meanwhile, combine the olive oil, flour, and poultry seasoning. Drain the potatoes and onions, reserving 1½ cups of the cooking water. Return the potatoes, onions, and 1½ cups of cooking water to the pan and cool slightly. Add the olive oil mixture, milk, cheese, and ham. Cook over low heat, stirring constantly, until the soup is thickened and the cheese is completely melted. Stir in the mustard.

Serves 6 to 8

CORN BISQUE WITH CHICKEN OR CRABMEAT

A wonderfully flexible recipe that can go one of two ways. If you choose chicken and chicken stock for this recipe, you will have a rich and satisfying soup that originated in Pennsylvania Dutch country and that will more than make a meal. If you use crabmeat and fish stock, the result will be very close to the famous New Orleans chowder that, according to legend, is a sure cure for a broken heart.

½ cup (1 stick) unsalted butter
½ cup all-purpose flour
¾ cup light cream or evaporated milk
2 cups chicken or fish stock, homemade (see page 25) or canned
1 can (16 ounces) corn, undrained
½ pound (about 2 cups) cooked chicken, or fresh lump crabmeat
1 teaspoon poultry seasoning, or ½ teaspoon liquid crab boil
   Chopped scallions, for garnish (optional)

In a medium saucepan, melt the butter over low heat until foaming. Increase the heat slightly, add the flour all at once, and cook, stirring constantly, 2 to 3 minutes, or until the flour begins to stick to the pan and colors slightly.

Add the cream or evaporated milk and the chicken or fish stock, whisking until the mixture is free of lumps. Add the corn, chicken or crabmeat, and seasoning or liquid crab boil.

Continue cooking, stirring occasionally, over low heat until the soup is heated through. Ladle into bowls and garnish with scallions, if desired.

Serves 4

SALMON BISQUE

Super easy and elegant, this soup gives all the satisfaction of a great chowder without all the fuss. Complement it with a crisp green salad and a good Chardonnay.

2 tablespoons unsalted butter
1 medium onion, coarsely chopped
2 tablespoons all-purpose flour
4 cups milk
2 cans (7 ounces each) salmon, drained and flaked with a fork
   Salt and freshly ground pepper to taste

In a medium saucepan, over low heat, heat the butter until foaming. Add the onion and cook until translucent. Add the flour all at once and cook, stirring constantly, until the mixture is browned, about the color of peanut butter, but not burned. Add the milk a little at a time, whisking constantly, and bring to a boil. Add the salmon and continue cooking until the soup is smooth and slightly thickened, about 5 minutes. Season to taste with salt and pepper.

Serves 6

MIXED GREENS BISQUE

Another recipe using greens of all kinds, this has a bisque-type base thickened with cornmeal or polenta. There is no real difference between the two, except that regular cornmeal is a finer grind of meal than the Italian-style grind of polenta.

¼ cup (½ stick) unsalted butter

4 cups mixed greens, such as dandelion, cabbage, collard, turnip, or mustard, washed and finely chopped

4 garlic cloves, peeled and pressed

2 leeks, white parts only, washed and finely chopped

1 carrot, scrubbed and grated

2 tablespoons all-purpose flour

2 cups milk

2 cups chicken or vegetable broth, homemade (see page 25) or canned

1 cup polenta or cornmeal mush, made according to package directions

½ teaspoon ground cumin

Salt and freshly ground pepper to taste

Place the butter in a large saucepan, add the vegetables, and lightly sauté over medium heat, stirring until the greens are wilted. Sprinkle the mixture with the flour and stir until well blended. Continue cooking an additional 2 to 3 minutes.

Add the milk and broth. Stir in the polenta or cornmeal until the soup is free of lumps. Add the cumin and salt and pepper to taste. Continue cooking until the soup is thickened, about 5 minutes.

Serves 6

OYSTER STEW

The perennial favorite for Christmas Eve, or any time you want elegance without effort. The use of canned smoked oysters in this recipe is rich and wonderful. And the soup does benefit from a good dash of sherry just before serving.

2   tablespoons unsalted butter
½   pint shucked fresh oysters, or 2 cans (6 ounces each)
      smoked oysters, drained
1   cup clam broth or juice
      Salt and freshly ground pepper to taste
1   cup half-and-half or light cream
¼   cup dry sherry (optional)
      Oyster crackers (optional)

In a medium saucepan over low heat, melt the butter. Add the oysters, broth or juice, and salt and pepper to taste. Simmer 10 minutes over very low heat. Add the half-and-half or cream and heat thoroughly, but do not boil. Just before serving, stir in the sherry, if using. Garnish individual servings with oyster crackers, if desired.

Serves 4

SEA SCALLOP SOUP

Like its close cousin, Oyster Stew, this classic for seafood lovers requires very little time or effort. Serve with oyster crackers or saltines.

    ¼   cup (½ stick) unsalted butter
    4   cups sea scallops
   1½   tablespoons all-purpose flour
    4   cups milk or light cream
        Salt and freshly ground pepper to taste

In a medium saucepan over medium heat, melt the butter until foaming. Add the scallops and sauté 3 to 5 minutes, stirring frequently to ensure even cooking.

Sprinkle the scallops with the flour. Blend lightly and continue cooking 2 to 3 minutes, or just until the flour begins to stick to the pan.

Gradually stir in the milk or cream and salt and pepper to taste. Continue heating over low heat for 10 minutes, but do not allow the soup to boil.

Serves 4

ACKNOWLEDGMENTS

Special thanks to Shirley Wohl for her dedicated editing, comments, and suggestions; to Pam Krauss and Anne Tamsberg for picking up where Shirley left off; to Kim Hertlein; to Susan DeStaebler and Howard Klein for their design expertise; to Sue Herner for her patience; and, of course, to the tasters—Andy, Linda, Gail, Mimi, and Jody and Jeffrey.

INDEX

Conversion Chart
Equivalent Imperial and Metric Measurements

American cooks use standard containers, the 8-ounce cup and a tablespoon that takes exactly 16 level fillings to fill that cup level. Measuring by cup makes it very difficult to give weight equivalents, as a cup of densely packed butter will weigh considerably more than a cup of flour. The easiest way therefore to deal with cup measurements in recipes is to take the amount by volume rather than by weight. Thus the equation reads:

1 cup = 240 ml = 8 fl. oz.   ½ cup = 120 ml = 4 fl. oz.

It is possible to buy a set of American cup measures in major stores around the world.

In the States, butter is often measured in sticks. One stick is the equivalent of 8 tablespoons. One tablespoon of butter is therefore the equivalent to ½ ounce/15 grams.

Liquid Measures

Fluid ounces	U.S.	Imperial	Milliliters
	1 teaspoon	1 teaspoon	5
¼	2 teaspoons	1 dessertspoon	10
½	1 tablespoon	1 tablespoon	14
1	2 tablespoons	2 tablespoons	28
2	¼ cup	4 tablespoons	56
4	½ cup		110
5		¼ pint or 1 gill	140
6	¾ cup		170
8	1 cup		225
9			250, ¼ liter
10	1¼ cups	½ pint	280
12	1½ cups		340
15		¾ pint	420
16	2 cups		450
18	2¼ cups		500, ½ liter
20	2½ cups	1 pint	560
24	3 cups		675
25		1¼ pints	700
27	3½ cups		750
30	3¾ cups	1½ pints	840
32	4 cups or 1 quart		900
35		1¾ pints	980
36	4½ cups		1000, 1 liter
40	5 cups	2 pints or 1 quart	1120

Solid Measures

U.S. and Imperial Measures		Metric Measures	
ounces	pounds	grams	kilos
1		28	
2		56	
3½		100	
4	¼	112	
5		140	
6		168	
8	½	225	
9		250	¼
12	¾	340	
16	1	450	
18		500	½
20	1¼	560	
24	1½	675	
27		750	¾
28	1¾	780	
32	2	900	
36	2¼	1000	1
40	2½	1100	
48	3	1350	
54		1500	1½

Oven Temperature Equivalents

Fahrenheit	Celsius	Gas Mark	Description
225	110	¼	Cool
250	130	½	
275	140	1	Very Slow
300	150	2	
325	170	3	Slow
350	180	4	Moderate
375	190	5	
400	200	6	Moderately Hot
425	220	7	Fairly Hot
450	230	8	Hot
475	240	9	Very Hot
500	250	10	Extremely Hot

Equivalents for Ingredients

all-purpose flour—plain flour
coarse salt—kitchen salt
cornstarch—cornflour
eggplant—aubergine

half and half—12% fat milk
heavy cream—double cream
light cream—single cream
lima beans—broad beans

scallion—spring onion
unbleached flour—strong, white flour
zest—rind
zucchini—courgettes or marrow

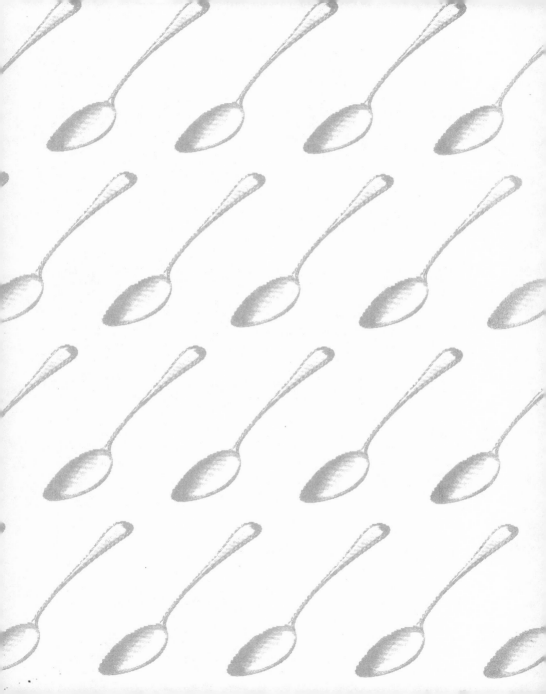

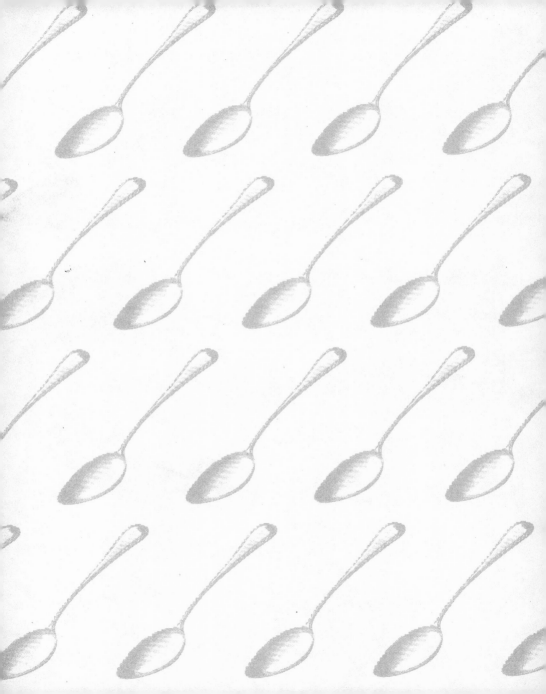